U.S. Sites and Symbols

★★★★★★★★★★★★

Capitals

Jennifer Hurtig

WEIGL PUBLISHERS INC.

Published by Weigl Publishers Inc.
350 5th Avenue, Suite 3304, PMB 6G
New York, NY 10118-0069

Website: www.weigl.com

Hurtig, Jennifer.
Capitals / Jennifer Hurtig.
       p. cm. – (U.S. sites and symbols)
Includes index.
ISBN: 978-1-59036-896-1 (hard cover: alk. Paper) – ISBN: 978-1-59036-897-8 (soft cover: alk. Paper) 1. United States—History, Local—Juvenile literature. 2. Capitals (Cities)—United States—Juvenile literature. 3. Cities and towns—United States—Juvenile literature. 4. State governments – United States – Juvenile literature. 5. Capitals—Juvenile literature. I. Title.
E180.H87 2009
973-dc22

2008015825

Printed in the United States of America
1 2 3 4 5 6 7 8 9 0   12 11 10 09 08

Editor: Danielle LeClair
Designer: Kathryn Livingstone

Photograph Credits

Weigl acknowledges Shutterstock, iStockphoto, and Dreamstime as the primary image suppliers for this title. Unless otherwise noted, all images herein were obtained from Shutterstock, iStockphoto, Dreamstime, and their contributors.

Other photograph credits include: Alamy: pages, 19 (bottom), 21 (top), 26 (bottom).

Every reasonable effort has been made to trace ownership and to obtain permission to reprint copyright material. The publishers would be pleased to have any errors or omissions brought to their attention so that they may be corrected in subsequent printings.

Contents

What are Symbols?

A symbol is an item that stands for something else. Objects, artworks, or living things can all be symbols. Every U.S. state has official symbols, or emblems. These items represent the people, history, and culture of the state. State symbols create feelings of pride and citizenship among the people who live there. Each of the 50 U.S. states has an official capital. It is called the state capital.

State Capital History

The state capital is the city where the state government meets. The capital is not always the largest or most populous city in a state. Sometimes, the state capital remained the same when the borders that defined the state were moved. Twenty-two state capitals have stayed a capital longer than the state because the territory, republic, or colony changed.

The oldest state capital is Boston, Massachusetts. It has been a capital since 1630.

Before 1800, eight U.S. cities, other than Washington, DC, have been the U.S. capital city.

Finding State Capitals by Region

Alaska

Hawai'i

Washington

Montana

Oregon

Idaho

Wyoming

The West

Nevada

Utah

Colorado

California

Arizona

New Mexico

Each state has a capital. In this book, the states are ordered by region. These regions are the West, the Midwest, the South, and the Northeast. Each region is unique because of its land, people, and wildlife. Throughout this book, the regions are color coded. To find a state capital, first find the state using the map on this page. Then, turn to the pages that are the same color as that state.

North Dakota

Minnesota

South Dakota

Wisconsin

Michigan

Iowa

The Midwest

Nebraska

Illinois

Indiana

Ohio

Kansas

Missouri

Kentucky

Oklahoma

Arkansas

Tennessee

The South

Texas

Mississippi

Alabama

Georgia

Louisiana

Florida

The Northeast

New Hampshire

Vermont

Maine

Massachusetts

New York

Pennsylvania

Rhode Island

Connecticut

New Jersey

Delaware

Maryland

West Virginia

Virginia

North Carolina

South Carolina

Web Crawler

Find out facts about each state at **www.americaslibrary.gov**. Click on "Explore the States."

The West

The West is made up of 13 states. They are Alaska, Arizona, California, Colorado, Hawai'i, Idaho, Montana, Nevada, New Mexico, Oregon, Utah, Washington, and Wyoming. Alaska is far to the north. It is separated from the rest of the country by Canada. The Pacific Ocean borders Alaska, Washington, Oregon, and California, and surrounds Hawai'i.

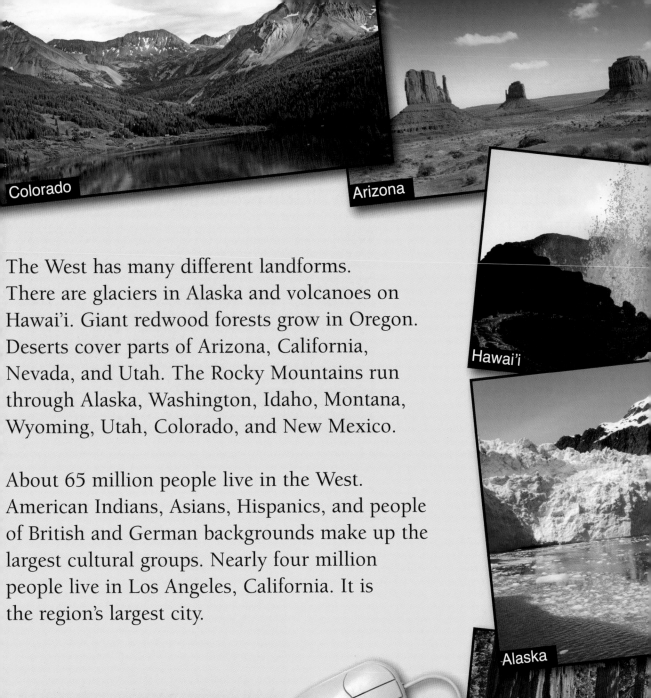

Colorado

Arizona

Hawai'i

Alaska

California

The West has many different landforms. There are glaciers in Alaska and volcanoes on Hawai'i. Giant redwood forests grow in Oregon. Deserts cover parts of Arizona, California, Nevada, and Utah. The Rocky Mountains run through Alaska, Washington, Idaho, Montana, Wyoming, Utah, Colorado, and New Mexico.

About 65 million people live in the West. American Indians, Asians, Hispanics, and people of British and German backgrounds make up the largest cultural groups. Nearly four million people live in Los Angeles, California. It is the region's largest city.

Web Crawler

Trace important events in the history of the West at **www.pbs.org/ weta/thewest/events**.

Discover the West's natural wonders by clicking on the states at **www.nps.gov**.

Alaska
Juneau

Juneau became the capital of Alaska in 1906. This city was named after Joe Juneau, who came to Alaska looking for gold in the 1880s. More than 30,000 people currently live in Juneau. It is the only state capital located on an international border. Juneau shares a border with British Columbia, Canada.

Arizona
Phoenix

Phoenix has been the capital of Arizona since 1889. Phoenix is located in the southern part of Arizona, and has a population of more than four million people. It is the U.S. state capital with the largest population.

California
Sacramento

Sacramento, named after the Sacramento River, became California's state capital in 1879. More than 450,000 people live in Sacramento today. It is located in the northern central part of California.

Colorado
Denver

Denver is located northeast of the center of Colorado. It has a population of more than 500,000. Denver was founded as a mining town, named after the former Kansas Territorial Governor James W. Denver. Denver became the state capital in 1876.

Hawai'i
Honolulu

Honolulu means "place of shelter" in the Hawai'ian language. It became Hawai'i's capital in 1845. When Hawai'i

became a state in 1959, many tourists started visiting. Besides Juneau, Alaska, Honolulu is the only state capital that is outside of the continental United States.

Idaho
Boise

Boise is located in the southwestern part of Idaho and has a population of over 200,000 people. This city became Idaho's state capital in 1865. Boise, sometimes called "The City of Trees," comes from the French word *boisé*, which means "wooded."

Montana
Helena

The state capital of Montana has been called Crabtown, Pumpkinville, and Squashtown. Finally, miners in the state chose the name Helena in 1889.

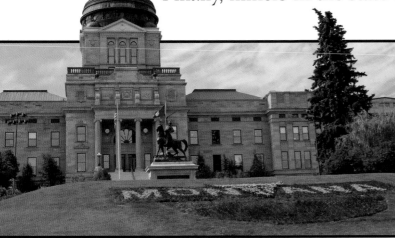

This city is located in the eastern part of Montana and has a population of about 25,000.

Nevada
Carson City

Carson City, with a population of about 55,000, is located on the western edge of Nevada. Carson City became Nevada's state capital in 1861. It was named after explorer Kit Carson. Besides Trenton, New Jersey, Carson City is the only capital city that borders another state. Carson City sits very close to the border to California.

New Mexico
Santa Fe

Santa Fe became New Mexico's state capital in 1610. It lies almost 7,000 feet above sea level, which makes it the capital with the highest elevation. This city has a unique layout. All buildings are built around a central plaza.

Oregon
Salem

Salem comes from Hebrew and Arabic words meaning "peace." It became Oregon's state capital in 1855. Salem has been nicknamed the "cherry city" because of the cherry-growing industry in Oregon.

Utah
Salt Lake City

Salt Lake City was nicknamed "Crossroads of the West." This was because of the mining and railroad industries found in the city at the time it was founded. More than 175,000 people live in Salt Lake City, which became Utah's state capital in 1896.

Washington
Olympia

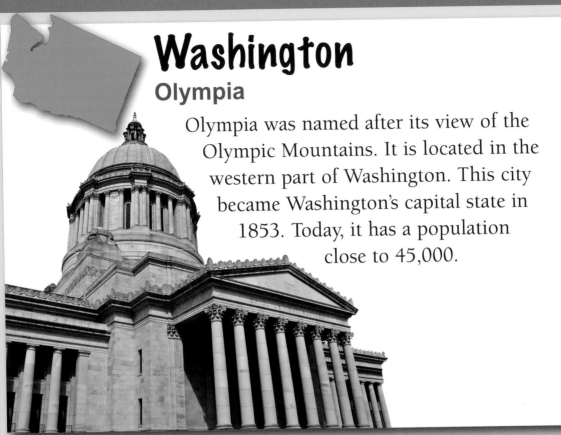

Olympia was named after its view of the Olympic Mountains. It is located in the western part of Washington. This city became Washington's capital state in 1853. Today, it has a population close to 45,000.

Wyoming
Cheyenne

Cheyenne, located in Wyoming's southeast corner, has a population of more than 55,000. It was named after the American Indian Cheyenne nation and became Wyoming's state capital in 1869. Cheyenne was well known for having large steam locomotives.

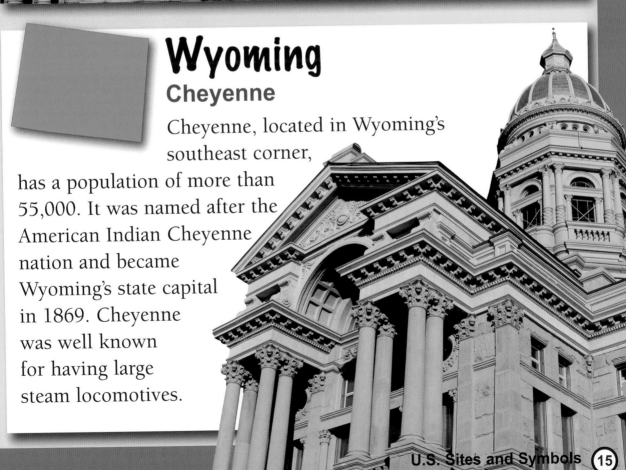

The Midwest

T he Midwest is in the center of the United States. It lies between the Rocky Mountains in the west and the Appalachian Mountains in the northeast. The Ohio River separates the Midwest from the South. Canada lies to the north. There are 12 states in the Midwest. They are Illinois, Indiana, Iowa, Kansas, Michigan, Minnesota, Missouri, Nebraska, North Dakota, Ohio, South Dakota, and Wisconsin.

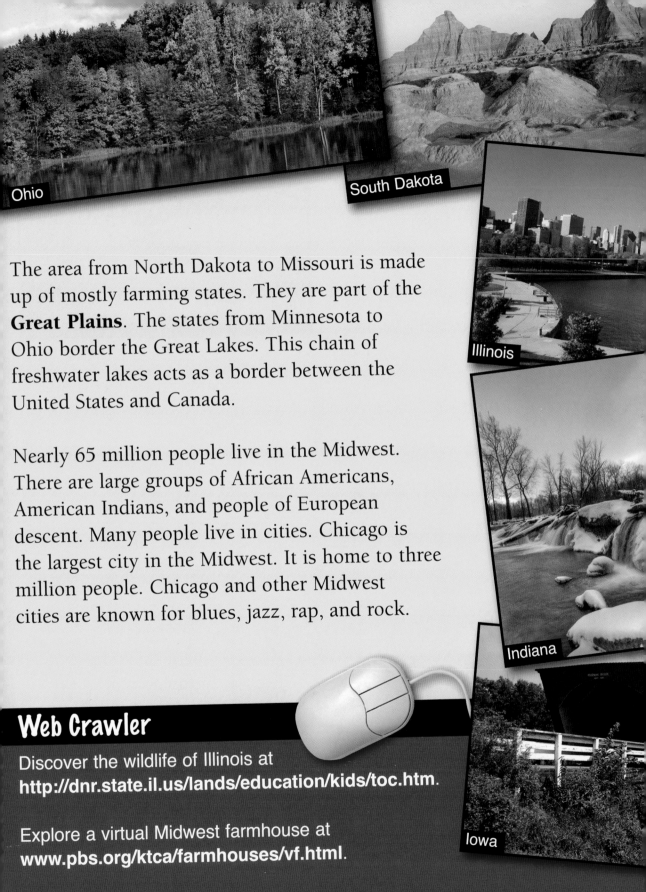

Ohio

South Dakota

Illinois

Indiana

Iowa

The area from North Dakota to Missouri is made up of mostly farming states. They are part of the **Great Plains**. The states from Minnesota to Ohio border the Great Lakes. This chain of freshwater lakes acts as a border between the United States and Canada.

Nearly 65 million people live in the Midwest. There are large groups of African Americans, American Indians, and people of European descent. Many people live in cities. Chicago is the largest city in the Midwest. It is home to three million people. Chicago and other Midwest cities are known for blues, jazz, rap, and rock.

Web Crawler

Discover the wildlife of Illinois at
http://dnr.state.il.us/lands/education/kids/toc.htm.

Explore a virtual Midwest farmhouse at
www.pbs.org/ktca/farmhouses/vf.html.

Illinois

Springfield

Springfield was originally named Calhoun after Vice President John Calhoun. The city was renamed Springfield and became Illinois' state capital in 1839. Abraham Lincoln moved to Springfield in 1837 and lived there for 17 years. The city is located in the central area of Illinois and has a population of more than 112,000.

Indiana

Indianapolis

Indianapolis, located in the center of Indiana, has a population of more than 785,000. The city became the state capital in 1821. It was named by Supreme Judge Jeremiah Sullivan, who combined the word *Indiana* with the Greek word *polis*, meaning "city."

Iowa
Des Moines

Des Moines became the state capital of Iowa in 1857. This city was founded in 1843 by Captain James Allen. He built a fort where the Raccoon and Des Moines Rivers meet. The city is located in the central part of the state and has a population of more than 534,000.

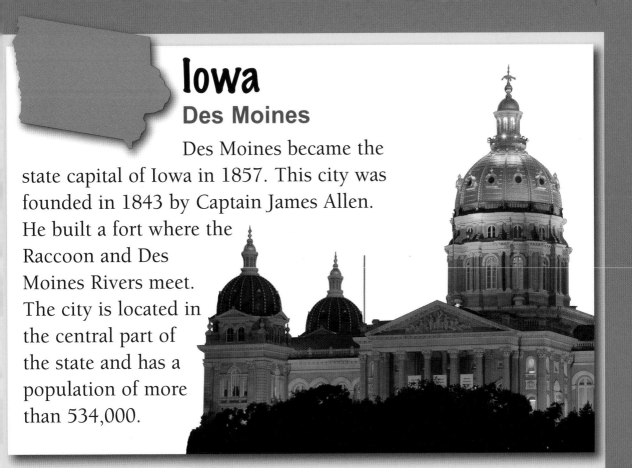

Kansas
Topeka

Topeka comes from an American Indian name which means "a good place to grow potatoes." The prairie potato was an important food for the American Indians that inhabited this area. This city became the capital of Kansas in 1856. Topeka is in the northeastern part of Kansas and has a population of more than 122,000.

Michigan
Lansing

Lansing is the only state capital that is not a county seat. This means that this city is not the **administrative center** for Michigan. In 1847, Lansing became the state capital. This city became the place where Olds Motor Vehicle Company began in 1905. It became an **industrial** center afterward. Today, more than 450,000 people live there.

Minnesota
Saint Paul

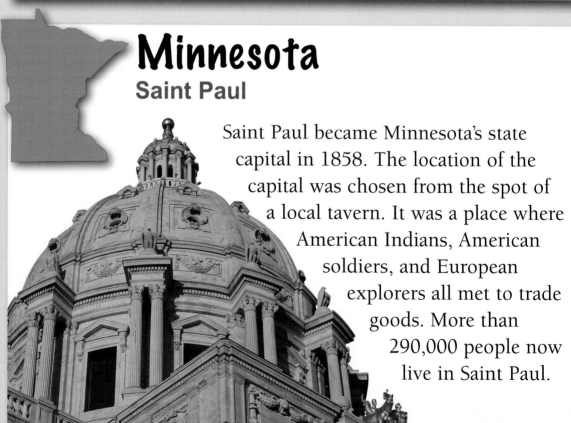

Saint Paul became Minnesota's state capital in 1858. The location of the capital was chosen from the spot of a local tavern. It was a place where American Indians, American soldiers, and European explorers all met to trade goods. More than 290,000 people now live in Saint Paul.

Missouri
Jefferson City

Missouri's state capital, Jefferson City, is located in the center of the state. Jefferson City has been the state capital since 1821. This city was named after the third president of the United States, Thomas Jefferson. When he was president, Thomas Jefferson signed the Louisiana Purchase, which made Missouri part of the United States.

Nebraska
Lincoln

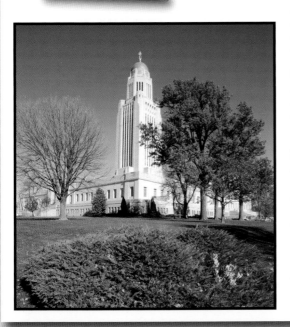

Lincoln, the state capital of Nebraska since 1867, was originally named Lancaster. Lancaster was renamed after President Abraham Lincoln was **assassinated**. The population of Lincoln is more than 225,000. The Nebraska state capitol in Lincoln is the second-tallest state capitol building in the United States.

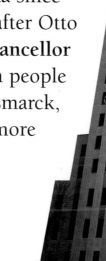

North Dakota
Bismarck

Bismarck has been the state capital of North Dakota since 1889. The city was named after Otto von Bismarck, a German **chancellor** who tried to attract German people to the area in the 1870s. Bismarck, which has a population of more than 55,000, lies in the southwest of the state.

Ohio
Columbus

Columbus, named after explorer Christopher Columbus, became Ohio's state capital in 1816.

Before this, there were disagreements as to which city should be the state capital, Zanesville or Chillicothe. Instead, the government made Columbus the capital because it is in the center of the state. The city has a large population of more than 710,000.

South Dakota
Pierre

In 1831, a representative of the American Fur Company named Pierre Chouteau, Jr., built a fur trading post he called Fort Pierre. When South Dakota became a state in 1890, the people of South Dakota were asked to choose the state capital. They could vote for Mitchell, in eastern South Dakota, or Pierre. When the votes were counted, Pierre had won by a large margin.

Wisconsin
Madison

Nearly 225,000 people live in Madison, Wisconsin's state capital since 1848. Madison lies in the southern area of the state and has many lakes within it or close by. Lake Mendota, Lake Monona, and Lake Wingra are all located near Madison.

The South

The South is made up of 16 states. They are Alabama, Arkansas, Delaware, Florida, Georgia, Kentucky, Louisiana, Maryland, Mississippi, North Carolina, Oklahoma, South Carolina, Tennessee, Texas, Virginia, and West Virginia. The Atlantic Ocean borders the South from Delaware to the tip of Florida. A part of the Atlantic Ocean called the Gulf of Mexico stretches from Florida's west coast to Texas. Mexico lies to the south.

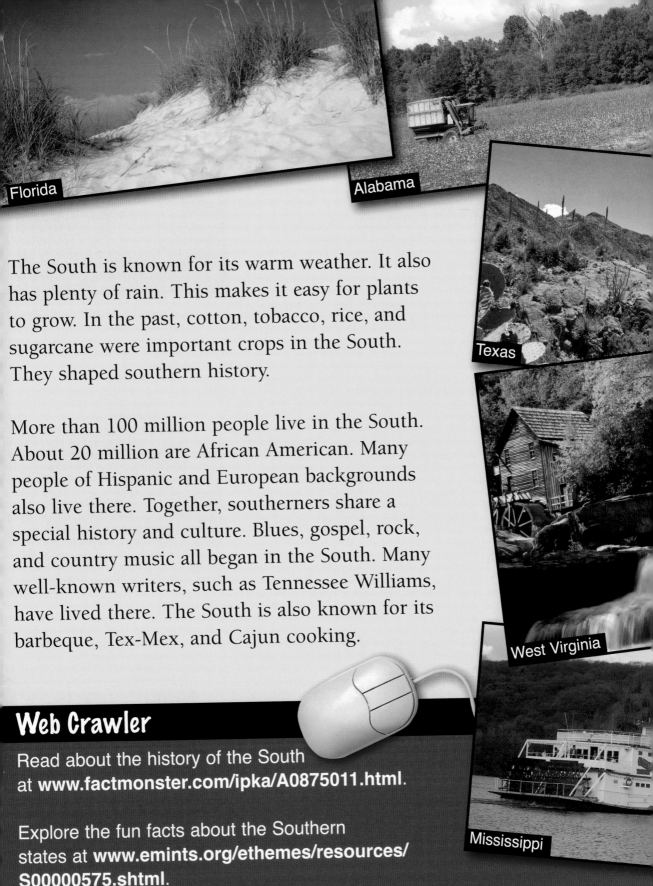

Florida

Alabama

Texas

West Virginia

Mississippi

The South is known for its warm weather. It also has plenty of rain. This makes it easy for plants to grow. In the past, cotton, tobacco, rice, and sugarcane were important crops in the South. They shaped southern history.

More than 100 million people live in the South. About 20 million are African American. Many people of Hispanic and European backgrounds also live there. Together, southerners share a special history and culture. Blues, gospel, rock, and country music all began in the South. Many well-known writers, such as Tennessee Williams, have lived there. The South is also known for its barbeque, Tex-Mex, and Cajun cooking.

Web Crawler

Read about the history of the South at **www.factmonster.com/ipka/A0875011.html**.

Explore the fun facts about the Southern states at **www.emints.org/ethemes/resources/S00000575.shtml**.

Alabama
Montgomery

Montgomery was the first capital of the Confederacy. This was a government formed by 11 southern states between 1861 and 1865. Montgomery became Alabama's state capital in 1846.

Arkansas
Little Rock

Little Rock, which became Arkansas' state capital in 1836, was named for a small rock formation that lies on the south bank of the Arkansas River. It was used to help guide people traveling down the river.

Delaware
Dover

Dover has been Delaware's state capital since 1777. Located in the center of Delaware, about 35,000 people live in Dover. The city was once the home of the American Revolution wartime leader Caesar Rodney.

Florida
Tallahassee

Tallahassee's name comes from an Muskogean Indian word meaning "old fields" or "old town." Tallahassee became Florida's state capital in 1824. The population grew significantly after World War II, as people moved to Tallahassee to attend university on the **GI Bill**.

Georgia
Atlanta

Atlanta is Georgia's fifth capital city. It became the state capital in 1868. Atlanta became well known during the Civil Rights Movement as "The City Too Busy to Hate." Atlanta has a population of more than 486,000 people.

Kentucky
Frankfort

Frankfort became Kentucky's state capital in 1792. The name Frankfort derives from "Frank's **ford**," an area where settler Stephen Frank died in 1780.

Louisiana
Baton Rouge

Baton Rouge, located along the Mississippi River, became Louisiana's state capital in 1880. More than 230,000 people live in Baton Rouge. This city dates back to the 1700s and has been the center of many wars and national movements.

Maryland
Annapolis

Annapolis has been the capital of Maryland since 1694. It became the temporary national capital in 1783. Today, more than 36,000 people live in Annapolis. This state capital is located on the eastern edge of Maryland, near Chesapeake Bay.

Mississippi
Jackson

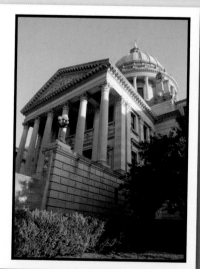

Jackson has been the capital of Mississippi since 1821. The city was named after President Andrew Jackson, in honor of his victory in the **Battle of New Orleans**. The population of Jackson is greater than 176,000.

North Carolina
Raleigh

Raleigh, well known for its many oak trees, is nicknamed "City of Oaks." Raleigh, which was originally called "Wake Crossroads," became the capital of North Carolina in 1792.

Oklahoma
Oklahoma City

In 1910, before Oklahoma was a state, the city of Guthrie was the territorial capital of Oklahoma. However, by 1910, Oklahoma City's population was more than 60,000. Many people felt it should be the state's capital. The people of the territory signed a petition to move the capital to Oklahoma City. There was no capitol building there, so until a building could be constructed, the government met in the Lee-Huckins Hotel.

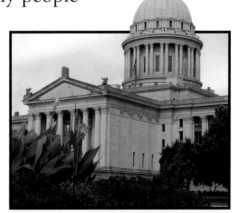

South Carolina
Columbia

Columbia was chosen as South Carolina's state capital in 1786 because of its central location. The city has many historical areas. The Robert Mills House and the Hampton-Preston Home have been restored so people can come relive the history of this city. The population of Columbia is more than 122,000.

Tennessee
Nashville

Nashville, also known as "Music City USA," became Tennessee's state capital in 1843. The Grand Ole Opry, a well-known music venue, opened in Nashville in 1926 and has helped make this city famous for its country music.

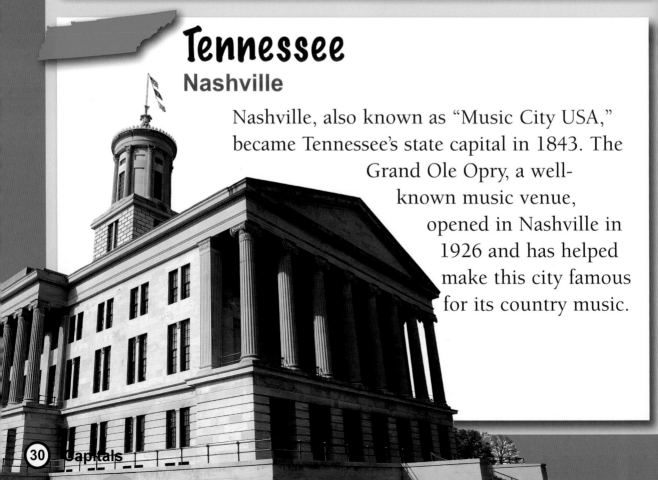

Texas
Austin

Austin has been the state capital of Texas since 1839. It is nicknamed "Silicon Hills" because of the many technology companies based there. The city is also nicknamed "The Live Music Capital of the World" because of its many musicians and theaters.

Virginia
Richmond

Richmond became Virginia's capital city in 1780. Virginia is the place where Thomas Jefferson wrote the **Virginia Statute for Religious Freedom** and where Patrick Henry gave the speech "Give me liberty or give me death."

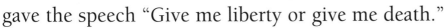

West Virginia
Charleston

Charleston, home to more than 50,000 people, became West Virginia's state capital in 1877. Charleston was an important part of West Virginia's growth, providing resources such as salt and natural gas.

The Northeast

The Northeast is the smallest region in the United States. It is east of the Great Lakes and south of Canada. The Atlantic Ocean borders the Northeast coast. There are nine states in the Northeast. They are Connecticut, Maine, Massachusetts, New Hampshire, New Jersey, New York, Pennsylvania, Rhode Island, and Vermont.

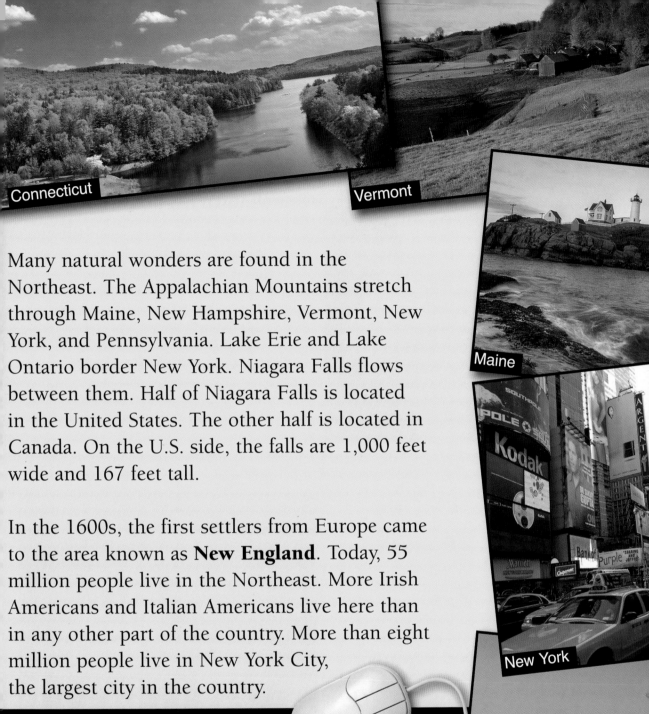

Connecticut

Vermont

Maine

New York

Pennsylvania

Many natural wonders are found in the Northeast. The Appalachian Mountains stretch through Maine, New Hampshire, Vermont, New York, and Pennsylvania. Lake Erie and Lake Ontario border New York. Niagara Falls flows between them. Half of Niagara Falls is located in the United States. The other half is located in Canada. On the U.S. side, the falls are 1,000 feet wide and 167 feet tall.

In the 1600s, the first settlers from Europe came to the area known as **New England**. Today, 55 million people live in the Northeast. More Irish Americans and Italian Americans live here than in any other part of the country. More than eight million people live in New York City, the largest city in the country.

Web Crawler

Learn more about New England at **www.discovernewengland.org**.

See spectacular views of Niagara Falls at **www.niagarafallsstatepark.com/Destination_PhotoGallery.aspx**.

Connecticut
Hartford

There are a couple of theories as to how Hartford received its name. One theory is that it was named after the British town Hertford. The other theory is that a settler, Stephen Hart had a crossing of the Connecticut and Park Rivers on his farm. The city was named after Hart's Ford. Hartford became Connecticut's state capital in 1875 and has grown to a population nearing 125,000.

Maine
Augusta

Augusta, named after Henry Dearborn's daughter, Augusta Dearborn, was made Maine's capital city in 1827. In the 1850s, Augusta was a mill town. It later developed as an important shipping center. The city has attracted more than 18,500 residents.

Massachusetts
Boston

Boston, which became Massachusetts' state capital in 1630, is a place of many firsts in the United States. It is the home of the first college, Harvard College, and the first subway systems. Boston also is the longest-serving state capital.

New Hampshire
Concord

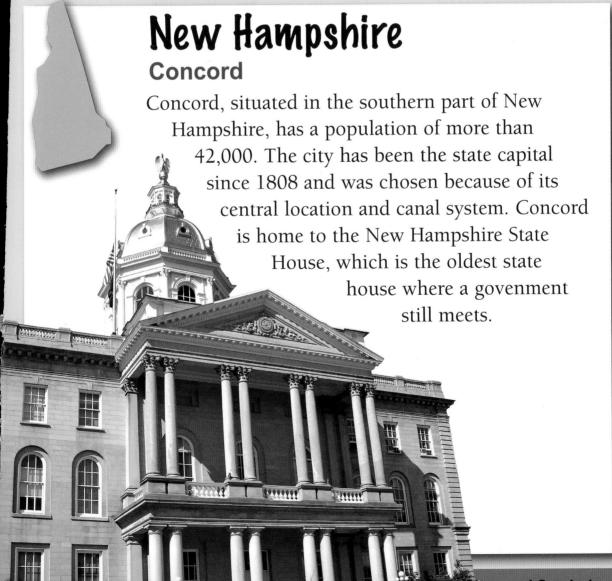

Concord, situated in the southern part of New Hampshire, has a population of more than 42,000. The city has been the state capital since 1808 and was chosen because of its central location and canal system. Concord is home to the New Hampshire State House, which is the oldest state house where a govenment still meets.

New Jersey
Trenton

Although Trenton has been the state capital of New Jersey since 1790, it was once the temporary capital of the United States. The city was named after William Trent, who owned much of the surrounding land. Trenton is where George Washington had his first military victory in the American Revolutionary War in 1776.

New York
Albany

Albany lies in the eastern part of New York. This was the site of the Dutch Fort Orange, and was named after James II, Duke of Albany. In 1777, Albany was chosen as the state capital of New York. It is the fourth oldest city in the United States and has a population of more than 94,000.

Pennsylvania
Harrisburg

Harrisburg was chosen as the capital in 1810. The first capitol in Harrisburg was destroyed by fire on February 12, 1897. The current capitol opened in 1906 and cost more than $12.5 million dollars to build.

Rhode Island
Providence

Providence, Rhode Island's state capital since 1900, is one of the first cities in the United States. It was one of the first cities to industrialize in the United States, with metal, jewelry, silver, and textile manufacturers.

Vermont
Montpelier

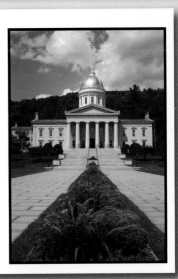

Montpelier became Vermont's state capital in 1805. It has the smallest population of all the state capitals. There are just more than 8,000 residents. European settler, Colonel Jacob Davis, named this city after the French city, Montpelier.

The National Capitol

National emblems are symbols that are used for the entire country. The American flag, known as the star-spangled banner, is one such symbol. Another is the bald eagle, which is the the national bird. The oak tree is the national tree. The national capital is Washington, DC.

The national capital is Washington, DC. The city was named after George Washington on September 9, 1791.

Washington was chosen as the country's capital in 1800 at a dinner hosted by Thomas Jefferson.

Washington is home to many national monuments, including the Jefferson Memorial, the Washington Monument, the Lincoln Memorial, and the Vietnam Veterans Memorial.

History of Washington

In March 1792, a contest was held to design the U.S. Capitol building. In all, there were 16 entries, but the government rejected them all. A late entry by William Thornton, an amateur architect, was accepted after the contest closed. The design had two wings united under a central dome. President George Washington liked the design because of its "grandeur, simplicity and convenience."

Guide to State Capitals

THE NATIONAL CAPITAL
Washington, DC

ALABAMA
Montgomery

ALASKA
Juneau

ARIZONA
Phoenix

ARKANSAS
Little Rock

CALIFORNIA
Sacramento

COLORADO
Denver

CONNECTICUT
Hartford

DELAWARE
Dover

FLORIDA
Tallahassee

GEORGIA
Atlanta

HAWAI'I
Honolulu

IDAHO
Boise

ILLINOIS
Springfield

INDIANA
Indianapolis

IOWA
Des Moines

KANSAS
Topeka

KENTUCKY
Frankfort

LOUISIANA
Baton Rouge

MAINE
Augusta

MARYLAND
Annapolis

MASSACHUSETTS
Boston

MICHIGAN
Lansing

MINNESOTA
Saint Paul

MISSISSIPPI
Jackson

MISSOURI
Jefferson City

MONTANA
Helena

NEBRASKA
Lincoln

NEVADA
Carson City

NEW HAMPSHIRE
Concord

NEW JERSEY
Trenton

NEW MEXICO
Santa Fe

NEW YORK
Albany

NORTH CAROLINA
Raleigh

NORTH DAKOTA
Bismarck

OHIO
Columbus

OKLAHOMA
Oklahoma City

OREGON
Salem

PENNSYLVANIA
Harrisburg

RHODE ISLAND
Providence

SOUTH CAROLINA
Columbia

SOUTH DAKOTA
Pierre

TENNESSEE
Nashville

TEXAS
Austin

UTAH
Salt Lake City

VERMONT
Montpelier

VIRGINIA
Richmond

WASHINGTON
Olympia

WEST VIRGINIA
Charleston

WISCONSIN
Madison

WYOMING
Cheyenne

Parts of the Capitol Building

The United States Capitol is among the most symbolically important buildings in the nation. It has housed the meeting chambers of the House of Representatives and the Senate for two hundred years. It stands today as a monument to the American people and their government.

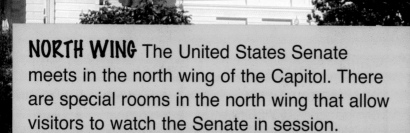

NORTH WING The United States Senate meets in the north wing of the Capitol. There are special rooms in the north wing that allow visitors to watch the Senate in session.

DOME A cast-iron dome, which is a large circular roof, tops the central section. A statue of a woman stands on top of the dome.

ROTUNDA The Rotunda is a circular room under the dome. This room is used for important ceremonies and events. It is more than 95 feet wide across the center of the circle, and 183 feet high.

NATIONAL STATUARY HALL This hall is found inside the Capitol. It contains statues of important Americans from the 50 states.

SOUTH WING The United States Congress meets in the south wing of the Capitol. Like the north wing, the south wing has rooms where visitors can watch Congress in session.

Test Your Knowledge

1 Which state capital has the smallest population?

2 Which state capital had three different names before its current name?

3 Which city is the only state capital that lies on an international border?

4 Of the cities listed below, which one is not a state capital of the Midwest?
a. Pierre
b. Albany
c. Des Moines
d. Columbus
e. Jefferson City

5 Which three cities have been state capitals for more than 300 years?

6 Which state capital city has the largest population?

7 Read the choices below. Which two state capitals cannot be reached by road?
a. Olympia and Tallahassee
b. Denver and Austin
c. Juneau and Honolulu
d. Phoenix and Providence

8 What is the national capital?

9

Which state capital is famous for its country music?
  a. Albany, New York
  b. Baton Rouge, Louisiana
  c. Nashville, Tennessee
  d. Austin, Texas
  e. Boise, Idaho

13

How many state capitals has Georgia had?

10

Which state capital has the highest elevation?

14

In what year was the last state capital adopted?

11

In which state capital did Abraham Lincoln live for 17 years?
  a. Springfield, Illinois
  b. Washington, DC
  c. Nashville, Tennessee
  d. Lincoln, Nebraska
  e. Little Rock, Arkansas

15

Which state capital was named after a formation that helped guide explorers down a river?

12

Which two state capitals were named after settlers' river crossings, or fords?

Answers:
1. Montpelier, Vermont
2. Helena, Montana
3. Juneau, Alaska
4. b. Albany, New York
5. Annapolis, Maryland; Boston, Massachusetts; Santa Fe, New Mexico
6. Phoenix, Arizona
7. c. Juneau, Alaska, and Honolulu, Hawai'i
8. Washington, DC
9. c. Nashville, Tennessee
10. Santa Fe, New Mexico
11. a.Springfield, Illinois
12. Hartford, Connecticut, and Frankfort, Kentucky
13. five
14. 1910, Oklahoma City
15. Little Rock, Arkansas

Create Your Capitol Building

Create a capitol to represent you. Begin by thinking about what type of capitol you want. Use this book to help you. What does the capitol in your state look like? Is the capitol in your state built in a place of importance? How will your design be the same as your state capitol? How will it be different? Where will you build your capitol? Will your capitol have a dome?

Think about how your capitol will look. Will it be large or small? Will it have a dome? Where would you put your capitol? Why? Look at the pictures in this book for help. You can also take a tour of the U.S. Capitol online at **www.senate.gov/vtour/index.html**.

Draw your capitol on a piece of paper. Use the diagram on pages 42 and 43 to help you design the parts of your capitol. Color your drawing with felt markers. When you are finished, label the parts of your capitol.

Write a description of your capitol. What kind of capitol is it? What does it say about you?

Further Research

Many books and websites provide information on state capitals. To learn more about capitals, borrow books from the library, or surf the Internet.

Books

Most libraries have computers that connect to a database for researching information. If you input a key word, you will be provided with a list of books in the library that contain information on that topic. Non-fiction books are arranged numerically, using their call number. Fiction books are organized alphabetically by the author's last name.

Websites

Find fun facts about each of the 50 U.S. states by clicking on this map from the U.S. Census Bureau
www.census.gov/schools/facts

Learn about the history of the Capitol at
www.visitingdc.com/capitol/capitol-building-address.htm

Read more about the regions of the United States at
www.factmonster.com/ipka/A0770177.html.

Find a map and take a virtual tour of the national Capitol at
http://clerkkids.house.gov/trip/capital.html

Glossary

adminstrative center: the place or building in which the government meets to run the state

assassinated: killed an important person by a surprise or secret attack

Battle of New Orleans: the final major battle of the War of 1812

chancellor: the head of state in Austria or the Federal Republic of Germany

ford: a shallow part of a body of water that may be crossed by wading

GI Bill: the GI Bill was part of the Serviceman's Readjustment Act of 1944. It provided a living allowance, tuition fees, and supplies for the higher education of veterans of World War II and the Korean War

Great Plains: a vast grassland region covering 10 U.S. states and 4 Canadian provinces. Used for farming and raising cattle

industrial: having to do with the making of goods and services

New England: the most northeastern U.S. states—Connecticut, Rhode Island, Massachusetts, New Hampshire, Vermont, and Maine

Virginia Statute for Religious Freedom: a law written by Thomas Jefferson and James Madison in 1797 that allowed the free practice of religion without discrimination

Index